Architects
at Home

Architects at Home

images
Publishing

Contents

Contents (continued)

Introduction

The scale of the single-family house is a building form that allows, and in many cases encourages, the architect to develop and test an idea or ideas that include or expand their own awareness of light, space, form, and context.

Architects use the design of their own homes both as an experiment and as a representation of their own beliefs and ideals. Their grounding through education, study, and personal experiences may form a base or starting point, but the influences of their culture, lifestyle, and the environment of their upbringing naturally form the design elements in their architecture. Architects' design positions are diverse, the context is diverse and cultures are varied. The customized house is a "one off," an architect's interpretation of design equated with the needs and values of their sense of a home. It is tailored to the architect's own family's program, and balanced by the architect's personal design perspective.

The size of an architect's own home is often an expression of their commitment to be more environmentally responsible and they scale the size of their home as a direct relationship to their needs. A home studio is where they can work and still be part of the family activities. The two-story living room with a mezzanine is being reduced in size or scale. A library of books may be replaced by the computer.

With the advent of the digital age, the future may be less defined. We can now be visually attached to our home without actually being there. Automation is changing the house in ways that we have not yet even thought of, and it will continue to do so. The new norm is change.

The rooms in a house are defined and your sense of the space reinforced by how the enclosure surfaces—the walls, floor, and ceiling—form and wrap the room or space.

The critical elements in defining or expressing a room are the floor and ceiling. Is the floor level, is the ceiling raised? A second critical element is the corners; the room is now contained, it has a boundary. Once the space is defined by the enclosure surfaces, the room is still not visible to the human eye without daylight or artificial light. How light is introduced into a room through openings in the exterior surfaces both defines the space and provides the room with its identity. By not placing the window on an axis with the door, this will initially contain your vision when you enter a room. You will experience the room before your eyes wander and recognize the architectural details or the furniture and other objects placed in the room. If you place windows in the corners of a room, a Frank Lloyd Wright trademark design element, as seen in the Freeman House, you eliminate one of the room's defining elements, thereby expanding the dimensions of a room.

The vertical dimension is also important. A tall or two-story room lifts your eye upward. A light source from above also unconsciously lifts your eyes upward, similar to the light source in a Gothic cathedral. This effect can be achieved in a modest manner by designing the natural light to enter the room through a skylight. This light source with inclined walls reflects the descending light into the room. The most dramatic example is perhaps the Oculus, (open skylight), in the Pantheon, Rome, where a disc of light transverses the space during the day. This movement of light introduces a sense of mystery or evokes a feeling of emotion as the light source, the sun, travels across the sky. In an interview Ricardo Legorreta discussed how natural light together with vibrant colors in his houses were designed to evoke a feeling of emotion. This is just a small part of the architect's vocabulary and dictionary of elements that create a room, a space, or a home.

The act of a person moving from one room to another or through a series of spaces, introduces the element of circulation. The primary element in circulation is where and how you enter the room, with the placement of the door or entry. By placing the entrance threshold at a corner, the diagonal view makes the room appear larger than it really is. By placing the door in the center, you achieve symmetry or balance. Even in an open-plan design, the point of entry is critical. Consider what it is that you first observe from this entry threshold.

A transparent or translucent skin provides a visual lightness and melds the form with the sky above or the landscape beyond. The boundaries of interior space are now expanded and exterior space captured. With walls of glass, the exterior space will extend the sense of the room. By way of example, in the Brick Country house designed by Mies van der Rohe in 1923, walls extend out into the landscape, thereby blurring the definition of where the interior ends and the exterior begins. In the Farnsworth house by Mies, the glass walls that wrap the house further blur the definition of the exterior, as the exterior wall becomes the landscape itself. Alternatively, instead of expanding out into the landscape, the house can partially or wholly contain an exterior space by surrounding the space and forming a courtyard or atrium. The courtyard, a traditional house form, expands the house by forming an additional room or space.

With the minimalist movement, clarity in the design of the room or space is seen as the dominant element. The addition of furniture may deconstruct the expression and power of the room as the objects in the space begin to cloud or reorient the focus. One can personalize the room with a fireplace, paintings on the walls, or the inclusion of a homeowner's own furniture. Occupying the room this way will provide that all-important sense of ownership.

The architect's palette and selection of materials is nearly endless, with the more traditional materials of concrete, stone, metal, wood, plywood, and glass, and the more flexible materials of plastic and plaster.

This palette is now supplemented with a fairly extensive list of new and composite materials. Infinitesimal designs and forms are now possible with this array of materials. But a material needs space to be appreciated or can occasionally be contrasted or highlighted with a second material. The traditional finished surface is usually smooth or an even texture, but now architects are exploring ways of modulating this surface, even with traditional tools, but also with 3D printing.

The moral responsibility today and in the future is to tread more lightly on the land to minimalize our personal consumption. Architects are at the forefront of this energy reduction and sustainable movement. The move toward the zero energy house is not solely technical but shows how responsible architects must be in the selection and use of materials that require lower energy and reduce air pollution in both production and maintenance. Placement of the house on a site is also important: is the house oriented toward the sun, to take advantage of the sun's heat when needed, but also protected from the sun with shading when the sun's heat is not needed. For example, Villa Girasol by architect/engineer Angelo Invernizzi, near Verona in northern Italy actually tracks the sun as the house rotates on wheels.

The architectural design elements that expand one's awareness of interior and exterior spaces and the iconic image of "home" are so diverse and numerous that the single-family house has become the archetype for the positive exploration of new spatial ideas and forms that reflect the various cultures and personal traits of the owners. The houses that follow represent a small segment of the designs that result from a successful collaboration between the architect as the designer and the architect as the owner.

John V. Mutlow, FAIA

Professor
ACSA Distinguished Professor
University of Southern California

An architect's home is a
reflection of themselves.

Their life, their values,
their experiences ...

DOMENIC ALVARO

NEXT
LEVEL
LIVING

Domenic Alvaro designed his award-winning Small House in an attempt to provide the solution to the limited footprint of an inner-city block—vertical zoning. As a practice of urban consolidation, Alvaro designed this home to ascend upwards, as opposed to extending outwards, by engineering multiple and flexible uses in each individual space.

The site measures only 20 by 23 feet (6 by 7 meters) at the base—about the same size as the garage of your typical suburban home—but stretches four stories.

The garage and storage facilities are located on the first floor, private spaces (bedrooms and bathroom) on the second floor, living areas on the third floor, shared spaces (kitchen, dining, entertainment) on the fourth, and a roof garden at the highest level, all accessed via a series of staircases. This stair space allows for air to be drawn from lower levels up through the rooftop sliding doors. The large sliding windows on each level offer further ventilation, and also maximize natural lighting and frame the Sydney skyline views. The perceived solidity of the external mass of the house provides privacy and thermal mass.

With this project, Alvaro considers a new architectural typology while reflecting a diverse and creative contemporary lifestyle, providing an affordable and sustainable option for inner-city living. Small House is an elegant, modern and simple response to the limitations of a very compact urban block.

MARLON AND MERYATI BLACKWELL

PERFECT BALANCE

The L-Stack House makes extraordinary use of an otherwise undeveloped but difficult plot—trapezoidal in shape and cut diagonally by a dry creek bed. Designed by architect duo Marlon and Meryati Blackwell, this exceptional home is immediately striking in its form, innovative bridging and stacking of volumes. It allows its resident family to connect with a sense of place that reflects the changing relationship between home, the urban setting, and the environment.

The prominent but compact one-story home comprises an L-shaped scheme of two 18-foot (5.5-meter) boxes hinged together, with one elevated and spun 90 degrees to maximize the space underneath and traverse the former creek. The first floor is structured as an open linear plan, with exterior terraces that connect the indoor spaces to the creek.

The windows and skylights provide natural lighting and privacy, with each one providing an intentional view of the external environment. Private spaces on the second floor are more enclosed and discreet, while the shared spaces are on the first floor. The interior is completed with wenge, walnut, and white oak millwork, painted wooden plank walls, and teak floors. Large steel boxes, inset into the walls and hallway, protrude on the exterior and are designed for sitting and sleeping.

The bulk of the exterior comprises an innovative rain screen made of rot-resistant Brazilian redwood. The end walls are constructed from either black metal cladding or glass storefronts, resulting in a well-balanced juxtaposition in the external aesthetic of the house.

OVER AND ACROSS

DAN BRUNN

When designing his own residence, Dan Brunn took matters a step further, and created a one-of-a-kind "bridge house" that literally cantilevers over a natural stream. The design exemplifies Brunn's signature minimalist aesthetic with a delightful choreography of light and volume that conveys drama and intrigue, while the design serves as a demonstration of innovative systems and forward-thinking processes.

Brunn found inspiration by the Vanderbilt family's former waterfront retreat, the Breakers in Newport, Rhode Island, particularly with the motor court and entry. Reworking the design by starting with a motor court, Brunn determined to evolve the structure of the residence and to straddle the stream rather than base the whole house on one side of the site.

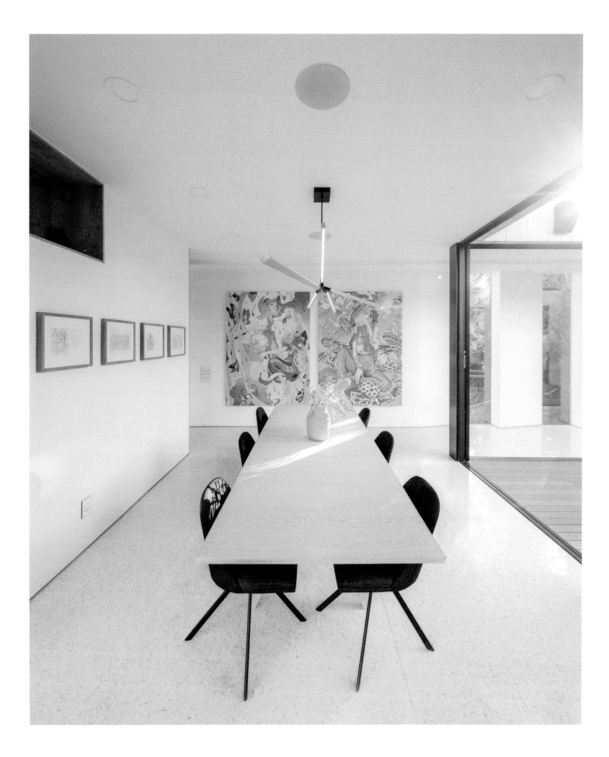

The waterway forms a natural division for public and private spaces in the residence, marking the point where one transitions into another. The public area in the front of the house comprises a double-height living room featuring a "Living Wall" of plants, dining room, kitchen, and den. Access to the outdoor terrace, with its lounge area and fire pit, is through floor-to-ceiling sliding glass doors, inviting the inside out, and the outside in. The exterior landscaping was carefully created to intertwine with the surrounding environment.

The private sector features a master suite with a walk-in closet and a sanctuary garden, as well as two bedrooms with a shared bathroom and one with an en suite.

Brunn conceived of the home as a net-zero home, with placement carefully positioned to avoid unnecessary heat gain while its length allowed beneficial northern exposure. Recycled steel was employed in the BONE Structure design. As a bonus, the bridge system resulted in less land being impacted. The pool is heated by photovoltaic panels on the roof, and a state-of-the-art home water system by Pentair with exceptional filtration. Bridge House is well-insulated, and internal air quality is enriched by the Living Wall of plants that helps to purify the interior air.

INTEGRATED WITH SITE

PAOLO CARLESSO

My trees are still twigs, my sons are still children, my house is not finished yet, there is still a little something to be done, everyday life is magic.

Paolo Carlesso

Architect Paolo Carlesso designed and constructed Casa CM, his own home, in an innovative and anticyclical way, in an attempt to radicalize techniques of architectural design. His design decisions were dictated by the use of sustainable materials and construction practices, with substantial financial benefits coming from the personal build, which was funded by the architect himself.

The modest house has a very simple design, with sophisticated and interesting elements precisely positioned throughout, including strong internal and external visual lines and juxtaposing blocks of raw materials. With gray external boards and an interior of rendered concrete and wooden paneling, Carlesso's design is both thoughtful and considered, and integrates beautifully with the site.

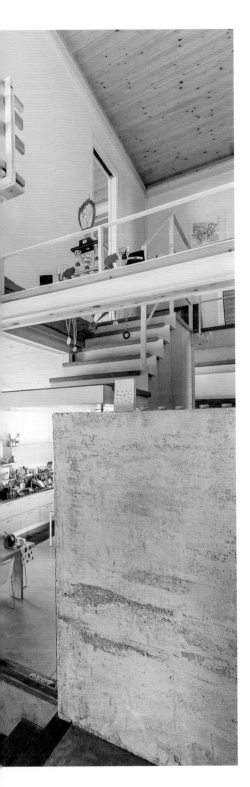

The structure features a steel frame covered by a ventilated exterior façade made from eco-fiber cement. The home's walls consist of interlocking timber panels, which have been assembled without the use of any adhesives. The history of the site has been purposefully enhanced by the architect's refusal to embrace the contemporary vernacular consistent with the region's urban expansion.

The organization of the site, the economy of the materials selected, and the self-construction of the building are all factors congruent with the period of re-colonization of the land that occurred at the hands of the immigrants in the mid-1990s.

MARK DE REUS

A NATURAL AFFINITY

This home for Mark de Reus and his family celebrates the career of its architect, who incorporated lessons from thirty-five years of practice into this, his most personal work. The home explores themes common to the firm's work as a whole—innovation, unpredictability, clarity of design, the use of natural materials, careful detailing and craftsmanship, and livability.

The home consists of the simple shapes of two practical building forms: a two-story agricultural barn form for the living areas, and an engaged flat-roofed structure for the garage, storage, and terrace. A two-story window lights the eastern entrance and stairway; it is designed to appear like a warm welcoming lantern on a dark night. Large windows on the western wall offer sunset views toward the Big Wood River at the rear of the lot.

To harmonize and complement the aspen forest setting, de Reus chose dark colors for the building's exterior: black-stained Douglas fir wood siding, graphite gray standing seam metal roof, black aluminum-clad windows, and black metal garage doors. The interior atmosphere is one of a modern cabin: with the use of rustic oak flooring, vertically applied white pine with a light finish that shows the grain but protects the wood from ultraviolet light.

Some of Big Wood Residence's details came as special requests from his family. De Reus's wife wanted a barn door, which he included in the powder room and garage, and his daughter asked for a window seat in her bedroom. Some of Mark's favorite details include the Alison Berger cast-glass dining light pendant, which speaks to the site's history as a place where block ice was cut from the natural springs for the Sun Valley lodge; the Peter Zumthor–designed light pendants over the kitchen island; the use of blackened and rusted steel alongside natural granite. One prominent detail—a steel shelf projecting from the fireplace mantel—was designed for a sculpture of Balinese Singa that de Reus acquired when he lived in Indonesia.

PHILIP M. DINGEMANSE

RAZZLE
DAZZLE

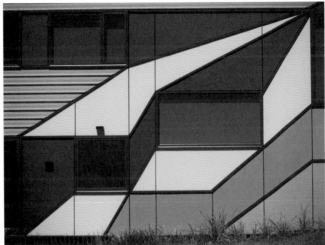

The playful and creative design of the outside, together with the internal spaces, is testament to the clever vision of Philip M. Dingemanse. This eminently personal home was designed with particular attention to the opportunities and consequences that arise when the owner is also the architect and builder.

Southern Outlet House adopts an early-twentieth-century technique in naval camouflage in order to allow the front façade to "dazzle." This not only manipulates the public-facing side, but also helps to adjust the home's scale. At night, the reflection of lights from the façade applies an extra dimension to an otherwise flat front, and defines the roof edge of the building. As a contrast to this external aesthetic, the interior timbers allow a textual warmth and open volume to the family's space.

Though reasonably small in floor area, all opportunities of the building section are maximized. As it is a steep site, the building is required to stretch across the sloping land with a continuous, straight roofline that eventually carries two stories underneath. Higher in the volume is a studio space that allows views across the living area. There are also opportunities for intimacy in this open space—a workbench shelters a sunken lounge below, forming a ceiling that allows privacy within the larger volume. With the addition of extensive gardens, light-filled spaces, sustainable architecture, and ample family space, Southern Outlet House represents the possibilities afforded when designing your own home.

MODERN RESILIENCE

TIMOTHY R. EDDY, FAIA

This Portland, Oregon, residence called Ash+Ash sits atop Mount Tabor, the only extinct volcano within a United States city. Owner-architect Timothy Eddy wanted to inspire others through uncompromised contemporary architecture that was seamlessly integrated with high-performance sustainable design.

In response to diverse weather patterns, the parti stems from a desire to create a range of terraces and porches for use at different times of the day. Central to the design concept is the desire to blur the lines between the outdoor spaces and the interior through extensive transparency, maintaining sweeping views of Portland and the surrounding mountains.

Expansive glass walls, an open plan, and strong horizontal lines draw heavily on Modernist influences. The L-shaped plan places main living and gathering spaces in a separate wing from guest and master bedroom spaces and encloses a visually private pool terrace. The core of the living wing is wrapped in rift-cut white oak and complemented by a cantilevered walnut stair to a rooftop viewbox. Interior walls and lighting are proportioned to display Eddy's collected artwork. Deep cedar soffits protect glazing from the sun and extend to the interior, forming a more intimate enclosure in the guest bedrooms, master bathroom, and rooftop viewbox.

The home boasts LEED Platinum certification, supported by numerous sustainable features, including a geo-exchange heat pump, under-floor radiant heating, rainwater recovery, and solar panels. This home is one of open space and sophisticated design elements.

GREG FAULKNER

HIDDEN AMONG THE WOODS

Designed in collaboration with Tom Kundig of Olson Kundig, Analog House celebrates a rugged, high alpine site. The home's footprint meanders through the understory, deliberately shaped to preserve existing specimen trees and create a protected internal courtyard.

Extensive transparency and clerestory windows throughout the home provide access to views and daylight, while numerous indoor/outdoor connections link the occupants to their surroundings. The interior palette features concrete and steel, including a steel mesh stair wall that works to providing visual and textural interest.

Dining room lights hang from custom bent steel armatures that organize and conceal electrical cords. A custom fireplace can be converted to an Argentinian grill.

The glass-walled "forest hall" connects the kitchen and dining wing to the living room and master suite with views of the surrounding woods on. Clerestory windows invite natural light into the interior, while a cantilevered steel roof provides cover for an exterior patio.

A discreet entry leads into the master suite, which includes an intimate sitting room, open casework closet, sleeping area, and bath. The custom bed, designed by Faulkner, faces the trees, while the master bath boasts a private view as well as a protected courtyard.

The "treehouse," a three-story tower, rises above the main volume of the home. The treehouse provides bedrooms and attached baths for guests as well as a roof-top deck with impressive views.

RAMBLE
ON

JON GENTRY, AIA

Located northwest of Seattle on the Kitsap Peninsula, this residence takes its place on a cherished piece of family property.

The program for the house was simple: three-bedrooms with space for playing music and drawing for a musician and an architect. The house is modest in size yet reaches into the landscape with a sheltering roof and screen walls to create usable outdoor spaces on all sides. The roof becomes an additional level for more occupiable outdoor space, including an elevated herb garden and star-gazing from the terrace.

Inside, the site-cast fireplace and chimney acts as a totem marking the heart of the living space—a space for family gatherings and music to be played.

The design concept evolved out of a solid rectangular volume in a typical one-story "rambler" style, sliced through and perforated to let in light and provide natural ventilation while maintaining privacy where needed. The ground plane with a raised concrete base performs multiple tasks as structure, heating source (radiant hydronic piping), and finish surface (polished concrete slab). The roof plane creates a large sheltering overhang that shades and protects the windows and provides space for a roof terrace, solar panels, and herb garden. The roof plane is carved away in select areas to open large voids and slices of skylights to allow light to wash walls and penetrate the main spaces.

The concrete base and full height masonry walls create a material language of visual mass and permanence for the home. The masonry walls and deeply raked mortar joints are highly textured, countering the smooth finished concrete surfaces and lime painted walls. The designers selected low-maintenance materials that would change with age while timber was milled on the site. Douglas fir trees were cut and dried in situ, and used in the finish lid of the roof plane as well as the open kitchen shelves and coffee table. Cedar milled on-site was used to create the entry door, entry benches, and east privacy fence.

Brick screen walls extend out into the landscape creating semi-enclosed exterior rooms that filter light and views, dissolving the structure into the landscape.

FOREST LOOKOUT

THOMAS GLUCK

New York–based architect Thomas Gluck designed this impressive structure as a vacation home for his family—as a stairway to the canopy of trees that fill this site in upstate New York. Tower House was designed with a simple objective—to build an energy-efficient, sustainable retreat.

Each of the first three levels comprises only one small, personal suite, with a modest sleeping space and bathroom. On the top level the living space stretches across the extension of the whole floor. An external deck on the roof of the house pushes the living spaces horizontally further into the canopy, allowing magnificent views of the mountains and lake.

A dual-sustainability strategy was implemented in order to improve temperature control. First, by organizing the wet zones of the house into an insulated central core, much of the house can be "turned off" when not in use. Second, the south-facing glass of the stairwell creates a solar chimney to take advantage of the stack effect to exhaust hot air out the top and draw fresh air through the house for natural ventilation. A key element of the design, the glass-enclosed staircase, also reflects back each layer of the rising canopy out to the observer. At night, with a few lights on inside, the house twinkles inside its surrounding treescape. With views of the Catskill mountain range, the house becomes both a lookout and a family retreat.

BUILDING FAMILY CONNECTIONS

SHAWN GOTTSCHALK

The Pavilion Haus is a calculated and thoughtful response to the economic and architectural questions surrounding how a young family might live.

The owners envisioned a home that would cater to efficiency, affordability, and flexibility. Adhering to a less is more concept, the project was designed as a pavilion with a focus on quality of space rather than size.

Exhibiting a strong connection to the outdoors, the home features planes of brick walls and floor-to-ceiling glass, with a back yard that opens up to a large covered deck and pool. The family enjoys being outside: a preference attributed to one owner's humble upbringings on a small farm. "Single-story living is critical to our family. It not only lends itself to a strong connection with the outdoors, but more importantly to each other," they say.

From the street the house reads as a modest and introverted design. A defined entry courtyard provides privacy from the street and a great place for the children to play.

Upon entry, through a large pedestrian gate that acts as a front door, the home begins to reveal its strong indoor and outdoor relationship. Blurring the boundary between the two was a key element in the home's design.

An open concept room includes the kitchen, living, and dining, and opens to a large covered patio, extending the living space outdoors.

ROBERT GURNEY

COURTING
IN STYLE

This small structure, sited in the rear yard of a residential property in northwest Washington, D.C., is designed to provide a small studio for the architect Robert Gurney to use, away from his main residence. The project also mediates between a gritty public alley and a landscaped rear yard with a swimming pool, resolving the unclarity. The addition of the new structure provides a private "courtyard" type space where the swimming pool and terrace are located. Studio 6420 itself is a simple rectangular volume with minimal fenestration. A tall chimney element is designed to accommodate all roof infrastructure in a single location and to provide access for both natural and mechanical ventilation. The building is covered with horizontal corrugated zinc siding to emphasize the length of the composition. A wood slatted fence is designed to be harmonious with an adjacent side garden while a Corten steel wall at the rear property line responds to the less refined alley context.

A small bathroom services the studio and provides a changing room for swimmers. The garage space, designed originally to house an automobile, proved to be a very flexible space. Soon after the structure was completed, the owner's son removed the car, inhabited the space and made it his own.

Gurney has created an efficiently designed addition, employing a simple, straightforward massing intended to provide a screen between the rear yard and the public alley. Studio 6420 is designed to be in scale with the courtyard it creates and the surrounding terraces and landscaping.

JOHN HENRY

LIGHT AND BRIGHT

The idea behind the design was to exploit the
daredevil and challenge the imagination.

John Henry

The award-winning Research House is situated in Research, a leafy Melbourne neighborhood known for its green belts and tree-lined streets. The original design was quite elaborate, an expansive tensile structure, which spanned much of the site. However, this was simply too expensive. Instead, an off-the-shelf shed was selected to act as the skeleton of the design, the walls of which were customized.

Inspiration for the design was drawn from architects such as Paul Rudolph and Robin Boyd. John Henry, the architect-owner, has a passion for the powerful connections between light and space and the dynamic relationship between intersecting floor levels. In response a series of platforms were created to seem to float above the natural ground in the shed, exposing the natural terrain below as well as Australian native shrubs and trees. There are very few walls, and the five open "rooms" are demarcated by changes in levels. A lot of the interior is exposed, creating a strong connection between all interior spaces and the outdoors. The southern façade is glazed, opening the inside to the bush beyond and elements from the external landscape have been incorporated inside the design, through the use of boulders, a pond, and the vast vegetation.

ISLAND ADVENTURES

JOE HERRIN

Boat trips to the San Juan Islands were the highlight of Heliotrope principal Joe Herrin's summers as a child. Through these trips he developed a love of boating and a deep connection to the San Juans—one that eventually led he and his wife Belinda to purchase a modest beach cabin on Orcas Island.

The cabin structure is a modest late-sixties-era kit A-frame. Over the course of their ownership Joe and Belinda have renovated as funds allowed—starting with the installation of a foundation, rebuilding the deck, and installation of insulated replacement windows (and insulation in general). Later they cut-in a big skylight and insulated the roof. Last year, nearing twenty years of ownership, they completed the renovation by addressing the kitchen and bath and creating a small addition off the back, which provided a much-needed entry and a comfortable shower. Solar panels were also installed to zero-out energy use. Their interventions have consistently focused on maximizing daylight, comfort, warmth and functionality, utilizing an economy of means.

Modest in scale, the cabin nevertheless regularly hosts multiple families comfortably by filling the loft and utilizing the tent platform out back. It functions as a social hub, hosting friends and family who return annually for summer weekends, and acts as a basecamp from which the family cycles, paddles, hikes, and cruises throughout the islands and north into British Columbia, Canada. The cabin also serves as a summer base for working away from the office.

Finishes are modest: reclaimed pine floors, birch-ply cabinetry with laminate countertop, original exposed fir structure finished with wood bleach, and beams painted to cover an original coffee-brown stain. Outside, siding consists of stained Tl-11 plywood, and the addition is clad in stained cedar milled on the island. There is a small garden on the south side providing summer salad ingredients, and a small shed behind for tools and toys.

CORTEN WITH CHARACTER

DAVID HOVEY JR., AIA

Arizona Courtyard House is a pavilion constructed with a system of standardized Corten steel structural components, and was built in under five months. The home demonstrates the flexibility of this sustainable building system to create a house of linear volumes, arranged to define a courtyard, with the main house to the south and east, a fitness center and lap pool to the north, and mountain views to the west.

It's set on a plinth of concrete that rises 16 inches (41 centimeters) above the terrain, used to redirect storm water around the house. The house is an open plan, based on a 7 by 7-foot (2.1 by 2.1-meter) modular system with columns spaced at 21-foot (6.4-meter) intervals on center. The two-way structural framing system allows for extensive cantilevers.

Corten steel was selected for its sustainable characteristics, and aesthetics, as its weathering is complementary to desert colors. The structural components are open to view, creating a contrast to the highly polished concrete floor throughout the house. The grid of beams overhead defines the ceiling and flows beyond the glass enclosure to create outdoor rooms in the courtyard, blurring the distinction between inside and out. Perforated, Corten roof panels allow filtered daylight from the sun to reach the courtyard below.

The exterior enclosure of the house is glass, with perforated sunscreens and press-formed louvers layered in front of the glass where shade or privacy is needed. This creates a sense of daylight at all interior spaces and rich texture of shades and shadows on the exterior.

Interior finishes were selected to achieve warmth. Extensive millwork of natural cherry, European oak and walnut is used throughout. Area rugs are placed on the polished concrete floor, with red MMA floor mats used at circulation areas. Draperies with high translucency create privacy while allowing light and views to the courtyard and mountains.

CRYSTALLINE FORM

FRANK JACOBUS

Like a mineral, the architecture of Hillside Rock emerges from interactions with its environment; an abstract outcropping situated within a lush forest. Located on a dramatically sloping site in the Ozark Mountains of Fayetteville, Arkansas, Frank Jacobus desired a home that would take advantage of the unique qualities of wooded enclosure and mountainous expanse the location offered.

The crystalline form is shaped in response to the desire to provide distinct views and experiences from each main living space. Three separate terraces are carved from an otherwise solid volume, each with a different perspective of the environment. The textured white envelope becomes a canvas that catches shadows from the surrounding landscape, revealing on its surface the complexity of forms that abound on the site while registering the changing character of light throughout the day. The façade's openings are choreographed to create singular connections to the land at different scales.

The interior's split-level organization is tuned to the hillside slope, animating an ever-changing section of cascading and nested spaces. A central wooden stair stitches together an intricate spatial section that transitions from a concrete base into sculpted white volumes whose scale mimics the immediate exterior environment, capturing the alternating exposure and enclosure found on the original untouched site. The interior is predominately white, so as not to compete with the beautiful cacophony of exterior colors as they change throughout the seasons.

BIRD'S-EYE
VIEWS

MARK AND ANGELA JAMISON

Architects Mark and Angela Jamison designed Bird House
on the Gold Coast in Queensland, Australia, as a home for
their young family. The home's unique design maintains a
strong connection to the site and its natural environment.
The site, which is surrounded by towering gum trees and
home to an abundance of native flora and fauna, takes full
advantage of the sloping, elevated landscape on which the
home is built. Anyone entering the upper living spaces
enjoys the feeling of being in a birdhouse among the
trees as the natural light and sounds of the forest canopy
penetrate the internal environment, with stunning views
to the trees, skyline, and famous Gold Coast hinterland.
All the while, privacy is maintained while still utilizing
the benefits of natural light and cross-ventilation afforded
by the passive solar design.

As a family, we feel connected to our environment and to each other within the home.

Mark and Angela Jamison

Essentially, the structure comprises two pavilions connected by a central grassy courtyard. By day, the courtyard offers shade and filtered light through the screens; by night, it frames the sky and provides a stunning outdoor room to spend time together as a family—watching films, or simply star-gazing. Operable screens can close the space or leave it open and connected to the surrounding landscape. The floor plan is efficient and retains a feeling of spaciousness with the use of floor-to-ceiling glazing. The result is an enjoyable space in which to spend quality time with their family.

DOUGLAS LARSON

COUNTRYSIDE
CHARM

Douglas Larson designed this house for his family, transforming and reviving a dilapidated old farmhouse. Sited on a stunning backdrop of Standfordville countryside in New York, the house was originally built in the late eighteenth or early nineteenth century. Numerous renovations had left no features of the original house so the design was not constrained to the usual limitations of a historical renovation, freeing Larson to design more personally. Elements harvested for re-use were the two-over-two windows, some clapboard siding, an antique bathtub, and old board doors. The effect is a gentle, handsome aesthetic that highlights the existing and new histories of the house, and is juxtaposed beautifully against the dark greens of the surrounding environment.

The existing, smaller interior rooms were replaced with larger spaces, and the structural beams and posts were exposed as an intentional design element. Of the previous wings of the house, the attic was removed to create a spacious family kitchen and common space, and the gable end wall was glazed all the way to the ridge. The former front porch was reinstated using Doric columns. The roof was also replaced with metal panels similar to nearby agricultural buildings. The existing materials were reclaimed wherever possible, and highly effective insulation techniques were used when replacing any walls and glass.

The Larson Residence has been imaginatively reinvented to bring a touch of modernity to a historical, picturesque property.

DAVID LIDDICOAT AND SOPHIE GOLDHILL

MAKER'S MARK

The Makers House is a new-build villa in Hackney, and a self-initiated project by husband-and-wife team David Liddicoat and Sophie Goldhill. Having bought the site in 2012, the architects won planning permission, raised finance, and built the house by hand as the main contractor over the following four years. They set their own brief to explore the ideal texture and atmosphere of domestic architecture.

Set within the Victoria Park Conservation area, the irregular site was constrained by neighbors' rights to light, and proximity to Listed Houses. Scrupulous computer analysis allowed the house's asymmetric form to be tuned to capture key moments of sunlight while forming apparently regular interior spaces.

The exterior combines roman brickwork with inky pigmented zinc roofing and bleached larch carpentry. Internally, the structural steel- and timber-work is exposed, and is married to a restrained palette of reclaimed and repurposed industrial materials.

Each room at ground level maintains a discreet atmosphere program, despite forming a highly connected living terrain. At the entrance level, the west-facing sitting room provides a formal space at a raised level. The whole rear façade is constructed from three large pivoting glazed doors (two which are full height) that open out to the courtyard garden. Stairs lead down from the kitchen to the basement where there is a dedicated utility room, larder, and television area.

Increasingly lightweight materials are deployed in the upper, sleeping levels, which are unified by a Rhodesian mahogany floor reclaimed from Hove Bus Station. The attic is conceived as a north-lit studio, while calm bedroom suites are arranged on the first floor. A paneled wall slides on cast iron to one side to define or amalgamate the bedroom and bathroom spaces. Expansive, bright circulations are designed to display art and family objects, or for occupants to enjoy moments of pause.

GROWING TOGETHER

ERIC LOGAN

Located on a sagebrush plain north of Jackson, Wyoming, Logan Pavilion is the family home of Eric Logan, Design Principal at CLB Architects, and his family. Originally built in 1997 on a tight budget, the minimalist home has adapted over time, evolving with the family's needs.

The home borrows its form from vernacular hay sheds. The gabled roof, held aloft on tall columns, is an appropriate symbol for shelter on the open plains and suitable for extreme weather conditions. The architect selected the exterior materials—cedar shingles, siding, and decking, as well as rusted sheet steel—for their ability to weather gracefully and blend with the colors of the landscape. Recycled and manufactured materials give the interior a contemporary feel. Oiled masonite wall paneling, raw MDF cabinetry, and an oiled concrete floor are economical interior finish solutions that allow the home to speak for itself.

My home is like a "new black sweater." The original
design has allowed the home to stand the test
of time, while also continuing to change.

Eric Logan

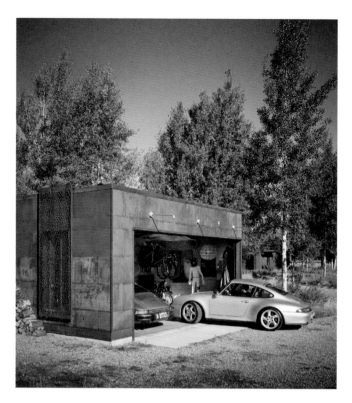

In 2001, the family added a guest house, which provides a space to host visitors, a yoga/workout room, and a space away from the main house. The property also grew to accommodate a garage, and later an addition to the garage, which houses Eric's many collections including cars, bikes, motorcycles, tools, and vinyl records. The garage forms are built from oxidized steel, which rusts and weathers with the surrounding climate.

Today, with a new remodel completed in 2020, the home comprises four bedrooms, three bathrooms, and a detached garage. This most recent iteration of the home includes a kitchen renovation, roof upgrade from a shingle roof to a metal roof, and new decking, siding, and stain. The new metal roof is a fulfillment of the original design concept for the home, which was met with strong opposition from the neighborhood design review and finally approved in 2020.

BOUND IN
A GRID

ANDREAS LYCKEFORS

On a southwest-facing slope by the sea stands Villa Timmerman, a semi-detached house designed by the married architect couple Andreas Lyckefors and Josefine Wikholm. The challenge was to create the house with equal qualities in both ends as they naturally face different directions, resulting in a careful study of local conditions. In the end the house could be arranged so that both parts of the house get sun in the morning, noon, and evening.

The stairs at the back of the house, with large windows and glass roofs, allow light deep into the ground floor and balance the large glass sections on the mezzanine level. Ceiling lights and the double-ceiling height help to create a home where the light flows even on cloudy days.

The couple wanted the house to be able to grow with the family and function well during all stages of life. By breaking up the conventional function-separated room plan, the floor plan can be given consistent qualities. The small children can sleep close to their parents while older children, teenagers, or guests can live on their own floor with toilet and their own living room.

The house is built entirely of wood, with a pre-fabricated frame that was mounted on-site. The dark wooden façade has been treated with wood tar, in a mixture of black and brown pigment. On the outside of the wood cladding are three grids of diagonal and vertical ribs. The grid was an experiment that proved to work well as extra protection against solar radiation on the façade and as a protective layer against the drifting rain on the west coast. The roof is a combination of tarred wood panel and solar cells. Here, the solar panels have been seamlessly integrated into the wooden roof.

CORBETT LYON

FOR THE LOVE
OF ART

The unique characteristic of the Lyon Housemuseum is that architect and art collector Corbett Lyon designed it specifically to provide the visiting public with a more intimate museum setting. This style allows the visitor to view the art in the context of the collector's own home, and draws its lineage from historical art museums, such as the Peggy Guggenheim Collection in Venice.

It appears as a "white cube" at the front of the building and a "black box" at its opposite end. Each spanning two stories, these volumes are expressed as anchors for the design. They are also creatively utilized as backdrops for the extensive collection of contemporary art installations. The first floor is expressed as a free-flowing space that transitions cleanly through the areas of the house and opens onto landscaped courtyards that showcase further artworks. The second floor is more private, with internal windows and slot-like openings from which the interior of the rest of the house can be viewed.

The walls and ceilings have small texts printed
onto the timber paneling. These reflect some
of the things that have interested us or have
been important to us as a family.

Corbett Lyon

Lyon confesses that living in the Housemuseum and opening it to the public is both challenging and rewarding. The project was awarded the Australian Institute of Architects' 2010 Harold Desbrowe-Annear Award for residential architecture, and in 2013 was named one of the World's 10 Most Exciting Buildings of Private Art Museums by art market company Larry's List. The Housemuseum represents a new and speculative architectural typology, and provides a novel way in which human beings can interact with art.

CHANGING THE MOOD

MARC MANACK

Mood Ring House is a very low-cost family home and
studio designed by architect Marc Manack. Situated in
an eclectic neighborhood of Fayetteville, Arkansas, the
design is a result of the limitations on-site, economic
constrictions, and programmatic desires. On the plot
are two prodigious Catalpa trees that Manack wished to
preserve. Other programmatic requirements included
orienting the house to take advantage of the northern
sunlight, while also maximizing the south and west
views of the forest and mountains.

A captivating feature of this T-shaped house is the lighting of the façades as night falls. Throughout the day, the house portrays a modest character despite its expressive form, a result of the gentle textures of the materials detailed to mask their humble character. In the evenings, the illuminated soffits create forms from the projected colorful LED light on the exterior and interior façades. These colors can be chosen by Manack and his family, creating a personal and kinesthetic connection with the space.

The studio areas of the home are consolidated on the first floor, with the majority of the family's living spaces concentrated on the second floor. The cantilevers and dramatic slope of the site give way to outstanding views of the natural, surrounding landscape. As such, the house is perfectly positioned in a private enclave among the trees; a private home with a vibrant public expression.

STACKING UP

ROBERT MASCHKE, FAIA

Robert Maschke, FAIA, took his inspiration for the striking architecture of C-House from the natural contrasts on this site. This house is a unique home in the Gordon Square neighborhood in Cleveland, Ohio, sheltering in a tranquil enclave within park-like land on its southern and eastern borders. With a beautiful tree-lined boulevard close by, and views of Lake Erie and downtown Cleveland, this design reconnects the site to its local environment.

Maschke utilizes a stacked program, providing each of the interior living areas with the best view possible. This sectional strategy results in a cantilever, which ensures that the exterior spaces below are sheltered, while also creating an intriguing element of architecture. Maschke employs a unique window system in order to resourcefully frame each of the views. The result is an expression that contrasts in opacity with each new elevation, with a differing character to its setting— nestled into the hill with its bold, white form. This unique structure has an iconic presence for anyone who has the privilege of passing by.

TERRY MCQUILLAN

WOOLOOWIN
WONDER

Located in the northern Brisbane suburb of Wooloowin in Queensland, Australia, Wooloowin House is a unique and bold extension to a traditional 1900s residential cottage. Architect Terry McQuillan intended to design a home that was sensitive to the heritage of the original building, while creating a space that his family could call their own. The front façade, historical in nature, is the result of McQuillan's sensitive refurbishment, which bears almost no resemblance to the home's dramatic extension. He and his wife were determined to create a new, strong connection with the outdoors and to maximize light, cross benches, and the available space beneath the house.

McQuillan's response is a weatherboard-clad, two-story extension separated from the original cottage by a louvered breezeway on the western side.

> The simplicity of the design and the transition space between the original house and the extension highlight the character of the old cottage.

Terry McQuillan

Incorporated in the addition is a new kitchen, a master bedroom, an outdoor living space at the upper level, and a gymnasium and carport at the lower level. The new addition boasts a strong connection to the outside, drawing in a significant amount of natural light and ventilation, the latter having a dramatic cooling effect on the home's internal temperature.

The extension has been crafted in such a way that it achieves a high level of privacy, despite the largely open-space planning. The sliding wall panels were designed to create partitions that closed off sections of the house not being used, ensuring privacy for the rooms while opening them up to the outdoors.

MARK MERER

NESTLED IN THE LANDSCAPE

Inspired by the placement, movement, and observation of natural elements, such as clay, sand, wind, and rain, Welham Studios searches for a triangulation of architecture, the environment, and our place between these two dynamics. Designed by architect Mark Merer for himself and his wife, artist Lucy Glenginning, Welham Studios was developed as an environmentally sensitive project that sits within its landscape, instead of above or beneath it.

The inspiration for this studio developed from a previous housing project conducted in collaboration with the Swinomish Indian Tribal community on Fidalgo Island in the United States. That project, entitled Landhouse, saw Merer working with collaborating architects to develop a "longhouse," a structure traditional to the Swinomish people, which actively interacts with the landscape. Encouraged by these constructions, Merer began to design a space that would interact this way with the English landscape. Welham Studios is assembled from insulated panels from the same Seattle-based factory that provided the materials for Landhouse. The design also utilizes Thermoform cladding, an EPDM-membrane roof with built-in root barrier, and a 4-inch (100-millimeter) substrate with a wildflower turf.

Welham Studios is a progressive design that incorporates deep-rooted housing traditions in order to negotiate the critical relationship between human beings and their environments. Nestled neatly and comfortably into the earth, the striking linearity of the design and color creates a studio that reflects Merer's creativity and open-mindedness.

PLANTING
NEW ROOTS

GEORGE THOMAS MIERS

Once their children completed college, architect George Miers and attorney Jenny Kuenster were confronted with a familiar dilemma—"downsizing" while maintaining a sense of "home" to which their children would wish to return. A magical 3-acre (1.2-hectare) property in Sonoma's historic wine region presented itself and became the perfect solution. While the existing house was tired, the land was large enough to construct an intimate family compound focused on indoor/outdoor living, and a large kitchen around which the entire family could gather for holidays and special events.

The resulting design integrated program and budget. The existing 2,200-square-foot (204-square-meter) home was largely gutted with the living/dining area rebuilt over the existing foundation to reduce costs. A centrally located kitchen addition with commanding views of the property was then introduced as the primary family gathering place while the overall exterior was integrated into a modern, indoor/outdoor living space featuring warm cedar siding accented against light cement-plaster walls and large planes of sliding glass doors. The bedroom wing was kept mostly intact with two bedrooms combined into one comfortable master suite and a reconfigured light-filled master bath opening onto a private rock garden.

Completing the "compound," the old garage was converted into a guest house and a new three-car garage with a one-bedroom apartment was attached, along with a pool and pool house, which together with the other outdoor living areas overlook a vineyard of syrah and roussanne.

ROMANCE IN THE DUNES

JETTY AND MAARTEN MIN

Jetty and Maarten Min designed Dune House, a highly unique and sustainable home with a striking appearance, to connect both form and materialization with the natural environment in which it is situated. Only 1,000 feet (300 meters) from the sea, the three-story house enjoys a dominant position on a dune crest in Bergen, in the Netherlands, where its tall, rounded form blends well with the neighboring dune and slender pine trees that guard it.

The oblique exterior façade and roof skin are formed from materials that create a balance with the romance of the scenery. Jetty herself designed a long, flat clay tile that matched these criteria, based on the Kolumba bricks designed by Swiss architect Peter Zumthor. The brown coloring of the British clay perfectly aligns with its surrounding environment. The eaves are finished with zinc to match the clay tiles, and the untreated wooden frames were handpicked for the longest sections to avoid as much adhesive as possible.

Openings in the roof surface were designed both as horizontal strips to capture views to the sea, and as one huge window to capture views across the dune, and the upper rooms of the house share different views of the dunes and sea.

IAN MOORE

COMPLETE CONTRAST

This deceptively simple and award-winning project is the conversion of a late-nineteenth-century former grocery warehouse in Surry Hills, Sydney, Australia into a two-level, one-bedroom residence.

Internally a 5 foot 6 inch (1.7 meter) height difference between the two streets is used to create the tall volume of the living space, with its floor-to-ceiling wall of books. The kitchen occupies the half level above, overlooking the living area and is screened by a black steel plate structure incorporating a built-in black leather bench seat. Tricky space requirements led to the adoption of the steel plate structure that flows through to the entry portals, the kitchen surround, and bookcase, virtually encasing the interior of the structure.

All existing structure has been retained, lined and painted white, while all new elements are painted black, a monochrome vision that perfectly highlights the owners' impressive collection of black-and-white photography. All joinery is finished in black anodized aluminum, including the bathroom on the upper level. The clear glazing allows light from the new clerestory window to illuminate the formerly dark center.

The main street façade reinterprets the original but in steel rather than timber, providing a contrast between the steel and the original brickwork, and completing the transformation from the nineteenth- to twenty-first centuries and from industrial to residential.

BOX OF TRICKS

RICHARD MURPHY

It sounds terribly egotistical, but I just
love living there and couldn't imagine
now living anywhere else.

Richard Murphy

Innovative and surprising, Murphy House occupies approximately half of an existing garden at the junction between two streets in the Edinburgh New Town.

Richard Murphy set out to achieve a number of architectural ambitions with his design. Firstly it acts as a "bookend" to resolve one of the four unsightly gables, the result of the development of two uncoordinated contiguous estates. The elevation continues the stonework pattern set up by the adjacent Hart Street houses. The dramatic sloping roof, made mostly of glass with inset photovoltaic cells, is designed to collect solar energy. The external form of the house is completed by a garage with a small roof terrace above which opens directly to the living space.

Internally an interlocking section places the living/dining and kitchen slightly higher on the second floor with the master bedroom at the apex. A study sits between the entrance hall and living room, and a bedroom is placed on the first floor and a further bedroom in a semi-basement. Mirrors are used to increase the sensation of space. The inspirations behind the house are many: principally, the work of Carlo Scarpa, Chareau's Maison de Verre in Paris, and the Sir John Soane Museum in London. The Australian architect Glenn Murcutt stayed here in 2015 and described the internal spatial configuration as a "Rubik's cube."

HOME
MADE

MICHAEL O'SULLIVAN

Michael O'Sullivan decided to design and build the O'Sullivan Family Home in a former working-class neighborhood, close to the Manukau Harbor in Auckland, New Zealand. Having grown up in South Auckland, O'Sullivan believes this to be one of the prettiest and most culturally diverse areas.

The home is a modest size and was a first-time build for O'Sullivan. He speaks of many challenges and a few tricky instances with an automatic nail gun throughout the build, revealing that even many years in the field do not always prepare you for your personal build. However, O'Sullivan's determination attracted the help of neighbors and friends who would spend their evenings helping with the build process.

Fabricated with a very minimal budget, the home is simple in plan and elegant in form. From the street, one enters through a courtyard shaded by oak into the main living pavilion, while laundry, bathroom, and bedrooms are positioned off a gallery to the back of the eastern deck. Light streams through slender windows and shutters.

O'Sullivan's countless hours spent on the build have allowed for strategic indulgences, such as exquisite green marble in the bathrooms, cedar weatherboard ceilings, and a shining brass kitchen island. Nestled in a beautiful area of Auckland, this open, welcoming, and highly personal design makes for a quintessentially coastal yet urban sanctuary for O'Sullivan and his young family.

SHANE PAVONETTI

RUSTIC
MODERNIST

The simple and sophisticated design of the Garden Street Residence in East Austin, Texas, harmonizes a pure Modernist style with the traditional barn and stable structures found throughout the United States. Designed and owned by Shane Pavonetti, this small home is a symbiotic collection of wrought aesthetic and rustic interiors—cedar siding, exposed wooden and steel framing, and steel windows, with the Modernist touch of spacious interiors, large windows, clean lineation, and trim-less detail.

A respect for the environment, as well as a celebration of the unpolished industrial textures of construction, is built into the very fabric of the house. The house boasts a handmade staircase, constructed on-site. The concrete slab foundation was left untouched on the lower floor, with tongue-and-groove framing lumber used as the final floor surface for the upper level.

The interior design is focused on showcasing the space with a simple elegance. The interior colors juxtapose dark features against light walls and floor, with additional elements kept as minimal as possible. Soft lighting, bold-colored furniture, and intentional placement of indoor plants soften the space and contextualize the house based on Pavonetti's personality.

CONCRETE
AMBIENCE

FERAS RAFFOUL

Skyline Drive 1 is the result of Feras Raffoul's many years in the architecture industry, combining the ideas that he had collected and admired over the years, with his passion for concrete as a single palette material. The result is this visually striking, three-story urban home with concrete forming the majority of the construction externally and internally.

Concrete, Raffoul believes, is a surprisingly warm material with efficient thermal massing qualities. The visual aesthetic of concrete, when absorbing and reflecting the shifting sunlight and external elements, creates a responsive, comfortable environment that is ever-changing. The glass roof takes advantage of the excellent views of the city of Melbourne, but it also allows the space to have a vast sense of scale as the boundaries of the interior and exterior are joined seamlessly.

The ambience of the house shifts and changes as light and dark penetrate the interiors through the glass roof throughout the day. The pool on the third level is a particular favorite of Raffoul's, with the acrylic wall introducing the pool into the internal living space.

Skyline Drive 1 is an exceptional use of the elements of water and sunlight on the internal and external aesthetics of a home. Raffoul's use of polished concrete appears softened and warm with the high levels of natural light, resulting in an outstanding, contemporary design.

I wanted to create as bare and minimalist
a design as possible.

Feras Raffoul

TRANSPARENT
INTENTIONS

THOMAS ROSZAK

Glass House, designed by Thomas Roszak, has a simple objective: to push the boundaries of everyday living into the future. Roszak's intentions were to build this home on a modest budget while at the same time providing a forward-thinking aesthetic with the space. This house experiments with transparency and reflectivity, while showcasing open, undivided spaces that are filled with natural light.

The home also needed to be built as an efficient smart house. With each variable of user-control to be reduced to the touch of a digital button (lights, shades, communication/audio, security, and air control), and the inclusion of a high-performance curtain-wall, the house has developed as a low-impact environment with advanced technological functions.

A planning module was developed that is based on a square room that measures 16 feet (4.9 meters) on each side. This "interstitial space" is utilized for hallways, bathrooms, and stairways, and ensures that the active rooms remain pure and uncluttered.

The trinity of sharp coloring—in the bright red lacquer, Brazilian cherry floorboards, and yellow steel— enables a warmth to exude from the interior spaces.

The house openly amalgamates the interior spaces with the exterior environment. The result is a very remarkable façade, where the mathematical calculation of the house design extends through into the layout of the wooded grounds. Roszak has succeeded in bringing elements of comfort and warmth to a unique, transparent space.

DAVID SAUNDERS

SALVAGED
FOR THE
FUTURE

Situated in St Kilda, Melbourne, architect David Saunders chose to revitalize a bayside heritage home for his young family by adding a new rear section. Saunders's aim was to leave the finished materials appearing as unchanged as possible—less white paint, more timber paneling, and natural or salvaged materials. Saunders was also the builder for the project, which enabled a hands-on approach, allowing him to evolve the design of the house throughout the build.

The front two rooms of the existing Victorian house were kept to maintain the existing heritage streetscape. With a level difference of 5 feet (1.5 meters) between the street and the higher rear lane, the new rear structure comprises ten changes in level. A number of those levels are wrapped around a central courtyard, which allows the early morning sun to brighten the house throughout winter.

The overall design is environmentally sophisticated, collecting over 11,360 gallons (43,000 liters) of rainwater in four basement tanks that supply water to the entire dwelling.

The design is also very personal, taking into consideration his collection of artworks, and incorporating bathroom gardens as part of the natural ventilation system. The roof level was designed to support 200 tons of soil, providing a productive "roof farm." Saunders brings panache and integrity to this complex and innovative home, which reflects his personal creativity in architecture and construction.

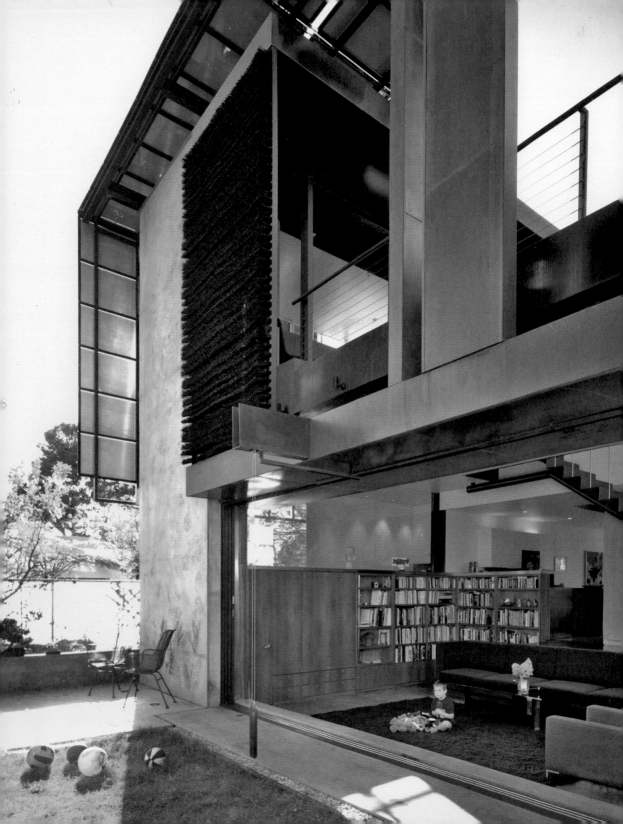

LAWRENCE SCARPA
AND ANGELA BROOKS

SOLAR
CANOPY

Inspired by Paul Rudolph's Umbrella House of 1953, the Solar Umbrella provides a contemporary reinvention of the solar canopy. The architects sought to take advantage of as many opportunities for sustainable living as possible with their design.

The original Californian bungalow is joined by a sizable addition to the south. Passive and active solar design strategies render the residence 100 percent energy neutral. A bold display of solar panels becomes the defining formal expression of the residence. Conceived as a solar canopy, these panels protect the building from thermal heat gain by shading large sections.

Exterior spaces are conceived of as outdoor rooms, and by creating strong visual and physical links between outside and inside, these outdoor rooms interlock with interior spaces, blurring the boundary and creating a more dynamic relationship between the two.

The master suite on the second level reiterates the strategy of interlocking space, strategically opening onto a deep, covered patio, which overlooks the garden, extending the bedroom area outdoors.

The architects take materials and contextually reposition them as design elements. Solar panels define, envelope, provide shelter and establish a distinctive architectural expression. Materials are selected for both performance and aesthetic value. The Solar Umbrella residence elegantly crafts each of these strategies and materials, exploiting the potential for performance and sensibility while achieving a rich and interesting sensory and aesthetic experience.

REFLECTING THE ENVIRONMENT

WERNER AND
URSULA SOBEK

Werner Sobek designed this extraordinary four-story home—named R128—on a steep section of land in Stuttgart, Germany. This home was designed to be completely recyclable, producing zero emissions, and functioning with 100 percent self-sufficient solar heating. Contributing to its highly striking appearance, this modular building is completely fitted with high-quality triple-glazing panels.

At maximum transparency, with glass panels comprising all four walls, the furniture has been kept very minimal with only a few pieces on each level. One enters the building via a bridge that adjoins the top floor. This top level contains the kitchen/dining space. The two levels underneath provide living and sleeping quarters, while the ground level includes the nursery and utility installations. The load-bearing structure of the building is a steel frame, reinforced by diagonals and placed on a strengthened concrete raft. All supply/disposal pipe networks and communication cables are protected within metal ducts that sit against the façade.

This highly sustainable model of architecture also employs a sophisticated digital energy system—ceiling panels filled with water absorb the heat/sun energy trapped inside the building. This heat is then relocated to a heat storage unit from which the entire home is warmed through winter through a reverse of this process. With such an advanced system of sustainability and glass panels that appear to be reflecting and absorbing the bright, verdant surroundings, this home sits modestly among and within its unique and beautiful environment.

JEFF STERN

ABSTRACTED FORMS

Skidmore Passivhaus is a simple, modern home in Portland, Oregon, that seamlessly merges high-energy efficiency standards with a contemporary design. Conceived as two connected boxes, the construction focused on efficiency and low cost. This 1,680-square-foot (156-square-meter) home is a certified passive house with an Earth Advantage Platinum rating.

The two-story space features an open plan with a loft-like master bedroom suite, while the single-story space incorporates two working studios and a shared bathroom. The space created between the volumes, while inside the thermal envelope, acts as an extension of the outdoor spacing connecting the front porch through to the rear deck. Boxy abstract forms remain clean and simple. Ballooned framed walls and roofs are clad in stained rough-sawn cedar.

The simple and sophisticated palette comprises concrete floors, white walls, and plywood cabinets, while brightly painted doors and laminate countertops provide sharp colors.

This passive home uses an airtight style of construction, coupled with triple-glazed European glass, an efficient heat recovery ventilator, and electric external aluminum shading that can be lowered to reflect heat gain. A high ratio of south-facing glazing maximizes solar gains for most of the year, while an extensive green roof helps manage stormwater, and provides habitat for birds and insects. Highly efficient lighting and appliances ensure that electricity usage is maintained at lowest possible levels, while a roof-mounted photovoltaic system generates about 75 percent of the home's annual power supply.

ROBERT SWATT

CONNECTING
ENVIRONMENTS

Swatt House, a 3,800-square-foot (353-square-meter) residence, is situated on a 1.5-acre (6,000-square-meter) north-facing site, overlooking a creek, mature oak trees, and the hills of a regional park beyond. The home includes a light and open interior suited to informal family life and entertaining, as well as a strong connection between the interior spaces and the natural environment.

The downwards-sloping site, with access at the top and flat land at the bottom, suggested that the site be broken into three functional areas: carport/studio, main house, and pool. By detaching the house from the carport and locating it roughly halfway down the slope, the lower level gains direct access to the pool while the upper levels enjoy full exposure to views and daylight from all sides.

The interior of the home is organized around a glazed south-facing two-story spine, which defines circulation, admits maximum daylight, and provides access to the entry courtyard. Spaces at the main "public" level are differentiated not through the use of walls and doors, but by materials, level changes, and built-in casework. To extend this openness to the exterior, five bi-folding glass doors open the spine and living areas to the entry courtyard, virtually eliminating the separation between indoor and outdoor spaces.

MICHAEL D. SZERBATY

DESERT
REFLECTIONS

Michael D. Szerbaty and his wife were attracted to the Verde Valley in Arizona by the unique crispness and clarity of the sunlight, which renders amazing colors and shadows on the rocks and vegetation. The steeply sloping site has stunning views of the Verde Valley, Sedona, and San Francisco Peaks. Morning Sky House, Guest House and Stable, incorporating earth-tone colors and natural materials, is designed to "disappear" in the landscape.

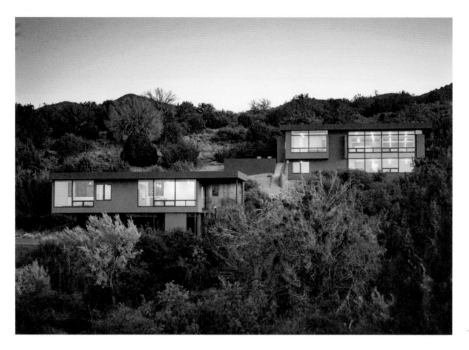

The main, 2,500-square-foot (232-square-meter) house is nestled into the land. The house is on two levels, with an open plan characterizing the upper level while the lower level is cut into the land with windows facing north. The upper floor contains the personal spaces and the main floor contains the transparent space of the living areas. A sky-lit open staircase connects the levels, allowing natural light and ventilation. Sitting separately, the horse stable and studio are similarly carved into the slope, with the 750-square-foot (70-square-meter) studio floating on pillars above the landscape and stable.

The large glass surfaces provide transparency, connecting inside to outside with a specific focus on views. The design for the house was inspired by American Indian ruins: ancient structures cut, carved into the natural landscape, and molded out of traditional materials. The intersecting geometries of the structures result in dynamic webs of woven grids. This project explores the meaning in such geometry overlaid on the spectacular natural landscape of the Verde Valley.

DAVID THOMPSON

CLEARLY
CONNECTED

With its three pavilions connected by a series of glass hallways, the single-story residence seeks to create a residential oasis in the heart of Los Angeles. Featuring camouflaged walls and an inviting open-air garden, the house stands in an isolated setting, with an indoor/outdoor spaces connection firmly established.

Comprising three low-lying volumes made from western red cedar cladding, glass, and dark cement board rooftops, the house is arranged around an outdoor courtyard and a back garden, with its surrounding area landscaped by gravel, paving stones, grass, and fauna, plus luxury amenities that include a pristine blue swimming pool. A deep overhang mitigates solar heat gain and shields from sun exposure.

A walkway of concrete pavers, lined by wild grasses leads to the front door, passing a tranquil courtyard with olive trees. The entry to the house is located within a glass hallway connecting the living pavilion to the west and the sleeping pavilion to the east.

The fluidity between the kitchen, breakfast room, and family room, designed for uninterrupted entertainment, creates a harmony of transparency and lightness. Instead of only externalizing interior spaces, exterior spaces are also internalized via pocket doors that fold into the walls. The grounds are interlocked with the interior space and the entire ensemble is activated by the purposeful arrangement of deeply layered sightlines, vignettes, and circulation connections.

Large windows, skylights, and pocketing doors infuse the home with natural light, reflecting off wooden floors and marble countertops. Complete with white-painted walls and ceilings, and pale wooden flooring, the house is littered with bold details such as black cabinetry and marble islands, which offset the interior's largely neutral palette.

Outside, the 40-foot-long (12-meter-long) pool and ample space create a series of outdoor rooms for outdoor entertaining. One of the main goals was to create an urban oasis and allow the living experience to engage with the property's natural landscape.

SLIPPING INTO PLACE

CARL TURNER

Slip House emerges as a striking sculpture in this busy Brixton neighborhood. This flexible, creative, and efficient use of space exemplifies the ability to design and build within a very constricted area and still achieve maximum logicality.

Slip House appears as three flexible "slipped" boxes that can be configured either as a single home, a studio workspace and apartment, or two separate apartments. The external walls are load-bearing, which ensures that no internal supports or beams are required. Additionally, the open plan of the interior spaces ensures that the walls are movable with minimal effort. Shared living and working spaces were particularly important, and this project allowed Turner to develop not only an exceptional home, but a home that formed a prototype for a new style of urban terraced house.

A key functional and aesthetic feature of the house is the translucent milky glass façade that provides cladding for the top level as well as creating a private enclosure for the roof terrace and an amazing quality of ever-changing internal light. It is also designed to Codes for Sustainable Homes Level 5, featuring ground source heat pumps, photovoltaic panels, a green roof, rainwater harvesting, under-floor heating, and mechanical ventilation heat recovery. Slip House is a prototype for efficient, flexible, and contemporary urban housing on a dense, limited site, and is a vehicle for the in-house research of future sustainable design.

Faced with no client except oneself, the project inevitably becomes a manifesto of sorts.

Carl Turner

CLIVE WILKINSON

HARNESSING THE VIEWS

The house program needed to accommodate two families coming together in a new home. The design furthermore needed to respond directly to its fortuitous hillside location hovering above the Los Angeles basin. Matching the two-story scale of its neighbors, the house is approached from the rear street and visitors descend into the front entry court. From there the vista opens up via an excision in the mass of the house and the view of the city emerges.

From the front door, visitors are drawn upstairs to a wide balcony to enjoy the view. The top floor is expressed as a large beamed attic space formed entirely in wood, with walls and soffits of sand-blasted Douglas fir and flooring in wide-plank white oak. Kitchen, dining and living, and working-from-home all co-exist. At the rear of this room is the enclosed library with custom black steel shelving. The exterior of this top-floor volume is clad in custom black zinc panels, emphasizing its role as the crow's nest.

With rough walls of sand-blasted concrete wrapping the first two floors, the house is nestled into the hill. These lower floors include five bedrooms and five bathrooms. The kids' rooms open onto the infinity pool terrace and the garden extends down the hill. The different levels address the varying family needs as children and parents can own their own territories but come together for social, recreational, and dining needs in one of the unique spaces created by the steeply sloping site: the living attic level, or the pool deck, or the garden terrace.

Credits

LAWRENCE SCARPA
AND ANGELA BROOKS
Solar Canopy 258–63
Brooks + Scarpa
brooksscarpa.com
Photography: Marvin Rand

WERNER SOBEK
Reflecting the Environment 264–69
Werner Sobek AG
wernersobek.com
Photography: Zooey Braun

JEFF STERN
Abstracted Forms 270–77
In Situ Architecture
insituarchitecture.net
Photography: Jeremy Bittermann

ROBERT SWATT
Connecting Environments 278–83
Swatt | Miers Architects
swattmiers.com
Photography: Russell Abraham

MICHAEL D. SZERBATY
Desert Reflections 284–89
MDSzerbaty Associates Architecture
mdsync.com
Photography: Jon Reis with Dede Hatch

DAVID THOMPSON
Clearly Connected 290–99
Assembledge+
assembledge.com
Photography: Matthew Millman

CARL TURNER
Slipping into Place 300–305
Turner Works
turner.works
Photography: Tim Crocker

CLIVE WILKINSON
Harnessing the Views 306–13
Clive Wilkinson Architects
clivewilkinson.com
Photography: Ema Peter

Published in Australia in 2023 by
The Images Publishing Group Pty Ltd
ABN 89 059 734 431

Offices

Melbourne
Waterman Business Centre
Suite 64, Level 2 UL40
1341 Dandenong Road
Chadstone, Victoria 3148
Australia
Tel: +61 3 8564 8122

New York
6 West 18th Street 4B
New York City, NY 10011
United States
Tel: +1 212 645 1111

Shanghai
6F, Building C, 838 Guangji Road
Hongkou District, Shanghai 200434
China
Tel: +86 021 31260822

books@imagespublishing.com
www.imagespublishing.com

Copyright © The Images Publishing Group Pty Ltd 2023
The Images Publishing Group Reference Number: 1670

All photography is attributed in the Credits on pages 316–19 unless otherwise noted. Page 2: Kevin
Scott (GO'C, The Rambler); Page 4: Kalle Sanner (Olsson Lyckefors Arkitektur, Villa Timmerman);
Page 12: Matthew Millman (Assembledge+, Laurel Hills Residence); Page 314: Scott Burrows (Jamison
Architects, Bird House)

A catalogue record for this
book is available from the
National Library of Australia

Title: Architects at Home (revised edition)
Author: John V. Mutlow [Introduction]
ISBN: 9781864709506

This title was commissioned in IMAGES' Melbourne office and produced as follows:
Editorial coordination Jeanette Wall, *Graphic design* Ryan Marshall,
Art direction/production Nicole Boehringer, *Senior editorial* Georgia (Gina) Tsarouhas

Printed on 140gsm Da Dong Woodfree paper (FSC®) in China by Artron Art Group

IMAGES has included on its website a page for special notices in relation to this and its other publications.
Please visit www.imagespublishing.com